Sheryl Webster
and Finger Industries Ltd present

and the Sheep

Zip and Zap went on a trip.
They went past the moon.

“Look at the green grass,”
said Zip.
“Let’s land on it.”

"Look at that!" said Zip.

"It is soft," said Zap.
"Let me sleep on it."

"No!" said the sheep.

“Look!” said Zip.
“It can go up there.”

“No!” said the sheep.

"It looks like a hat," said Zap.

"No!" said the sheep.

"Look at the rain," said Zap.
"Let me get under it too,"
said Zip.

"NO!" said the sheep.

"You can not get under me.
You can not sleep on me.
I can not go up.
I am not a hat!"

"Oh no!" said Zip.

“We must go,” said Zap.

"This is for you," said Zip.
"Goodbye!"